SPOTLIGHT ON SOCIAL AND EMOTIONAL LEARNING

THE RIGHT THING TO DO

ETHICAL RESPONSIBILITY

DAVID MACHAJEWSKI

PowerKiDS press™

NEW YORK

Published in 2020 by The Rosen Publishing Group, Inc.
29 East 21st Street, New York, NY 10010

Editor: Rachel Gintner
Cover Design: Michael Flynn

Photo Credits: Cover Nattapong Wongloungud/EyeEm/Getty Images; cover, pp. 1, 3–4, 6, 8, 10, 12, 14, 16, 18–24 (background) TairA/Shutterstock.com; p. 5 Steve Debenport/E+/Getty Images; p. 6 Kdonmuang/Shutterstock.com; p. 7 https://commons.wikimedia.org/wiki/File:The_Boy_Who_Cried_Wolf_-_Project_Gutenberg_etext_19994.jpg; p. 8 StockImageFactory.com/Shutterstock.com; p. 9 Aaron Amat/Shutterstock.com; p. 11 (main) Pavel_Klimenko/Shutterstock.com; p. 11 (inset) frank_peters/Shutterstock.com; p. 12 marekuliasz/Shutterstock.com; p. 13 Andrey_Popov/Shutterstock.com; p. 15 Chelsea Guglielmino/Getty Images; p. 17 Chicago History Museum/Archive Photos/Getty Images; p. 18 Prostock-studio/Shutterstock.com; p. 19 ogichobanov/Shutterstock.com; p. 20 Ursula Page/Shutterstock.com; p. 21 patpitchaya/Shutterstock.com; p. 22 simon jhuan/Shutterstock.com;

Cataloging-in-Publication Data

Names: Machajewski, David.
Title: The right thing to do: ethical responsibility / David Machajewski.
Description: New York : PowerKids Press, 2020. | Series: Spotlight on social and emotional learning | Includes glossary and index.
Identifiers: ISBN 9781725306844 (pbk.) | ISBN 9781725306875 (library bound) | ISBN 9781725306851 (6pack)
Subjects: LCSH: Responsibility--Juvenile literature. | Ethics--Juvenile literature. | Values--Juvenile literature. | Conduct of life--Juvenile literature.
Classification: LCC BJ1451.R24 M3525 2020 | DDC 179.9--dc23

Manufactured in the United States of America

CPSIA Compliance Information: Batch #CWPK20. For further information contact Rosen Publishing, New York, New York at 1-800-237-9932.

CONTENTS

CHAPTER ONE

DECISIONS, DECISIONS

Picture this—you have a big team project due tomorrow. Your role, or part, is to write a report about your team's work. You begin writing the first sentence, and suddenly the phone rings. One of your friends is inviting you to go see a movie you *really* want to see. You start to walk out the door, but you suddenly get an uncomfortable feeling in your stomach. Going to the movies would be awesome, but what will happen if you show up to school without a report?

You have control over your actions during tricky situations like this one. When you consider the consequences your actions will have on other people or things, you're on your way to ethical responsibility. Ethical responsibility is the ability to make choices that benefit not just you, but also other people and the world around you.

Some studies show young people make over 3,000 decisions a day. Decisions can be easy, such as choosing what to eat for lunch, but others are much harder.

CHAPTER TWO

UNPACKING ETHICAL RESPONSIBILITY

Growing up comes with many responsibilities, such as helping clean up after meals or completing homework on time. But what makes a responsibility ethical?

Remember the story of the boy who cried wolf? The moral of this story is clear—lying usually causes more harm than good.

The word "ethics" relates to decisions about whether certain actions are right or wrong. When you make a decision that has to do with ethics, your morals are put to the test. You might remember the word "moral" from fairy tales or other stories. Many of these stories have a moral, which in this case means a lesson, at the end. Usually, honest and brave characters are rewarded, and dishonest or greedy characters are punished. A person's morals or ethics are the ideas that lead someone to behave one way or the other.

Even though fairy tale endings are uncommon in real life, these stories teach us something important. Ethical responsibility involves making choices between right and wrong.

CHAPTER THREE

GO WITH YOUR GUT!

If you ever wonder whether a situation calls for ethical responsibility, a good course to take is to pause and check how you're feeling. Just as your stomach growls around lunchtime, or you get goose bumps when you feel scared, your body gives signals when situations require you to make a choice between right or wrong.

For example, a queasy, or nervous, feeling in your stomach can signal that you feel worried. Breathing faster, sweating, or feeling restless—which are part of the body's "fight or flight" response—are common responses to dangerous situations. These signs are your body's way of telling you to slow down and really consider the effects of your actions. Your body can't force you to make the right decision, but we all have a feeling for right and wrong. Your feelings provide clues about the ethics of a situation.

Nervous habits—such as chewing your fingernails—are also signals that you may feel worried about a situation.

CHAPTER FOUR

LET YOUR VALUES BE YOUR GUIDE

Understanding when situations call for ethical responsibility is a good step toward making the right choices. Choosing between right and wrong can still feel **intimidating**. When it comes to moral decisions, there isn't usually a single "correct" answer. Instead, everyone must make decisions based on their opinion of what is fair and right.

Your character, or how you think, feel, and behave, can help guide you toward the best course of action when you're faced with tricky situations. Every person has a **unique** character guided by different values. Although everyone has their own set of values, there are three key **aspects** of character considered very important to ethical responsibility. These values are: **integrity**, **compassion**, and **citizenship**

In the next few chapters, we'll explore what these three values mean and why they matter when it comes to ethical responsibility.

At its heart, your character is the sum of who you are and how you act. The choices you make, and how you approach the world, make up your character.

CHAPTER FIVE

THE MEANING OF INTEGRITY

Imagine you're riding your bike down the street. You spot something that looks out of place—a wallet on the ground! You open it and see a lot of money. You also notice a driver's license, or permit, belonging to your neighbor. What do you do next?

When faced with a **dilemma**, ask yourself what feels fair. You might think, "I found this wallet, so now it belongs to me." But even if that feels fair, does it feel honest? Would you be comfortable telling your parents or friends that you took the wallet? Probably not.

Even though you might want to take the money, the person who lost it would certainly miss it. Returning the wallet would be the fair and honest thing to do. By doing so, you would be showing integrity. Integrity means doing the right thing, even when no one's watching.

Have you faced a dilemma recently? Think about your first thoughts, the people involved, and your final decision—how did you make your choice?

CHAPTER SIX

COMPASSION COUNTS

Having compassion for others is a bit like having a superpower. It encourages you to spring into action when someone needs your help.

Compassion looks different depending on the dilemma at hand. For example, if you see a classmate being left out of an activity, using compassion could mean inviting them into your group. You can also show compassion for the world around you. For example, picking up trash in your community is a form of compassion. By doing so, you **simultaneously** protect the environment and care for those who live in your neighborhood.

No matter the situation, when it comes to ethical responsibility, compassion counts. When you respect the needs and feelings of others, you're guiding your actions in an ethical way. And when many people behave ethically, it makes the world a better place.

Compassion doesn't just have to apply to other humans. Jane Goodall (middle) is a groundbreaking **researcher** who has helped people understand how animals think and behave. She has shown compassion throughout her life as someone who cares about animals' well-being.

War

CHAPTER SEVEN

CITIZENSHIP: DOING YOUR PART

While there are laws that determine whether an individual is a lawful citizen of a country, citizenship has another meaning. Citizenship also means being actively involved in the **betterment** of society.

There are many ways to be a responsible citizen. Volunteering, or offering up your time and effort for a cause you feel strongly about, is a great way to be responsible. Staying informed about important issues is another way to do your part. The more you understand an issue, the more informed your decisions will be. Adults can be responsible by voting in elections. They support candidates and issues that match their ethics.

Being a responsible citizen means doing your part to improve the lives of those around you. Citizenship is a way of being ethically responsible for all of society, instead of just your friends and family.

Ida B. Wells showed strong ethical responsibility through her reporting. By looking into and writing about terrible treatment against African Americans, Wells helped bring injustice to light.

CHAPTER EIGHT

ETHICAL DECISIONS: CHARACTER IN ACTION

Understanding how to make ethical decisions is important. But ethics involves more than understanding—it requires taking action.

Ethical dilemmas are easier to solve with a plan. So the next time you think a situation calls for ethical responsibility, try taking these steps.

Asking the five Ws early in the ethical decision-making process helps you review your choices.

1. **GET THE FACTS.** Ask the five Ws (who, what, where, when, and why).
2. **THINK ABOUT THE ISSUE.** What seems right, or fair, in the situation? What seems wrong, or unjust?
3. **GAIN PERSPECTIVE.** Try imagining the situation through another person's eyes to understand their **perspective**.
4. **WEIGH THE CHOICES.** There's often not a perfect way to deal with an ethical dilemma. Ask yourself: "Which choice will create the most good, and the least harm, for everyone involved?"
5. **CHECK YOUR CHARACTER.** Ask yourself, "Which choices match the most with my values?"
6. **MAKE A DECISION.** Use your best judgment to make a decision.

CHAPTER NINE

LEARNING FROM MISTAKES

Sometimes, ethical responsibility can feel like a **burden**. We all make mistakes, so it's hard to always act ethically. Focusing on our own needs sometimes causes us to take actions that might be selfish or unfair. If you find yourself in a situation where you could have been more ethically responsible, don't get too upset. Instead, do your best and try again next time.

Learning from your mistakes will make you a stronger decision-maker in the future.

There will be times where you thought you made very ethically responsible decisions, but your decisions didn't have a good outcome. Someone's feelings might have been hurt, or someone might have become angry. In these situations, it helps to ask yourself what you could have done differently. Sometimes, no matter what you did, the outcome wouldn't have been perfect.

CHAPTER TEN

KEEP ASKING QUESTIONS

Ethical dilemmas can be some of the trickiest situations out there. As you read this book, you may have asked yourself, "Do I have what it takes to be ethically responsible?"

The answer to this question is simple: yes! When you're in doubt about how to approach an ethical dilemma, let your thoughts be your guide. Think about the values that are important to you, and measure those values against possible actions. If you behaved a certain way, would you be acting with integrity? Would you consider your actions compassionate? Would you be doing your part in your community?

The answers to these questions may not always be yes, but that's OK. Ethical responsibility takes practice, and making mistakes along the way is part of the process. Remember, while it's important to have compassion for others, it's just as important to have compassion for yourself.

You have what it takes to be ethically responsible.

GLOSSARY

aspect (AZ-pekt) A part of something.

betterment (BEH-tuhr-muhnt) The act of improving something.

burden (BUHR-duhn) A duty or responsibility.

citizenship (SIH-tuh-zuhn-ship) The status of being a citizen, or the work someone does to be a good citizen in a community.

compassion (kuhm-PAA-shuhn) Kindness, wanting to help others.

dilemma (duh-LEH-muh) A situation in which you have to make a hard choice.

integrity (in-TEH-gruh-tee) The quality of being honest and fair.

intimidating (ihn-TIH-muh-day-ting) Causing feelings of fear, uncertainty, or anxiety.

perspective (puhr-SPEK-tiv) Point of view.

researcher (ree-SUHR-chuhr) Someone who does research, or careful study to find new knowledge.

simultaneous (sy-muhl-TAY-nee-us) Happening at the same time.

unique (yoo-NEEK) Special or different from anything else.

INDEX

PRIMARY SOURCE LIST

Page 7
"The Shepherd Boy and the Wolf." Illustration. Milo Winter. From *The Aesop for Children*. Published 1919.

Page 15
Jane Goodall, center, at the Los Angeles Zoo. Photograph. Chelsea Guglielmino. September 23, 2018.

Page 17
Ida B. Wells. Photograph. 1920. Now at the Chicago History Museum.

WEBSITES

Due to the changing nature of Internet links, PowerKids Press has developed an online list of websites related to the subject of this book. This site is updated regularly. Please use this link to access the list: www.powerkidslinks.com/SSEL/ethical